Hi, I'm Jada!

SHEVONICA M HOWELL

JARROD L. WALLACE JR
JEREMIAH K. WALLACE
JADA L. WALLACE

Illustrated by Farrah Prince

To order additional copies of this book, contact:
Xlibris
844-714-8691
www.Xlibris.com
Orders@Xlibris.com

ISBN: Softcover   978-1-6641-8079-6
         EBook   978-1-6641-8078-9

Print information available on the last page

Rev. date: 06/26/2021

Hi, I'm Jada ...

This is my family!

My Mom is Ms. Jazmine,
but you can call her Ms. Jazz.

My Mom's favorite color is Royal
Blue, and she loves to bake.

My Dad is Mr. Jarrod, but you
can call him Big J-Rod.

My Dad's favorite color is Red,
and he loves his family.

I have two Big Brothers ...

Jarrod and Jeremiah

Jarrod is my oldest brother,
and his favorite color is Red.

You can call him Lil J-Rod.

My youngest brother is Jeremiah,
and his favorite color is Blue.

You can call him King.

My full name is Jada Lyric
Wallace, but you can call me
Jada Bae, Petunia of Poochhh,
or my favorite, Lil Boss Lady!

My favorite color is Purple.

We are the Wallace Family,
but you can call us J5!

About the Authors:

Jada is a 3-year old that love to dance. She wants to get into gymnastics and her birthday is in August.

Jeremiah is 8-years old, he will start third grade in August 2021, and his birthday is in September.

Ms. Howell is a mother and grandmother of two. She is the Founder & CEO of Academy of Scholars, Inc., she is the Literacy Coach of JaxPAL in Jacksonville, Florida, and her birthday is in November.

Jarrod is 9-years old, he will start 4th grade in August 2021, and his birthday is in October.

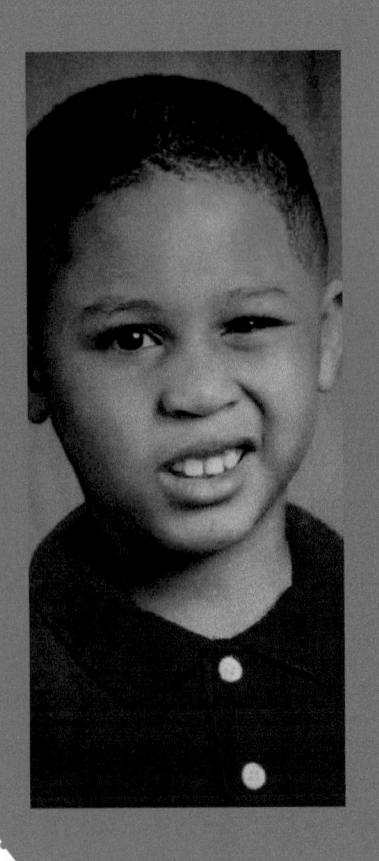

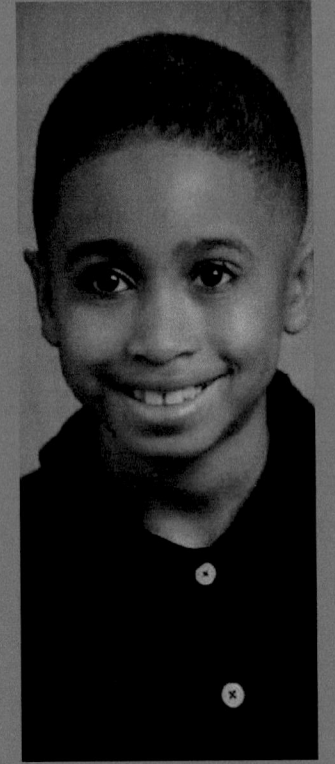

Books Related to this title:

Girl, they Ain't Ready! (2011)

I CAN DIG SIS ... THEY AIN'T READY! (2017)

What's in a Name? (2018)

A Play With Words Word Search (2020)

The "YOU TEACH IT" Study Guide (2020)

We Love You, Dre? (2021)

A is for Audre' ... (2021)

Te'Rana Aliyah ... A BEAUTY WITH BRAINS! (2021)

Finding Myself ... AM I ENOUGH? (2021)

WORD SEARCH

JADA	JEREMIAH	JARROD	BIG J. ROD	JAZZ
MOM	DAD	BROTHERS	SISTER	RED
BLUE	LOVE	PURPLE	PRETTY	BEAUTIFUL
HANDSOME	SCHOOL	BAKE	PLAY	LOVES

B	M	O	M	Y	T	T	E	R	P
H	E	Q	K	S	C	H	O	O	L
A	J	A	R	R	O	D	R	J	B
N	B	P	U	R	P	L	E	A	R
D	L	F	L	T	S	M	D	Z	O
S	B	A	K	E	I	W	A	Z	T
O	X	L	V	J	S	F	D	Y	H
M	U	O	A	K	T	N	U	A	E
E	L	D	Z	F	E	V	O	L	R
H	A	I	M	E	R	E	J	P	S
E	U	L	B	I	G	J	R	O	D

IS
LOVE
LOVES
MOM
NAME
OF
OTHER
OUR
PLAY
PRETTY
PURPLE
RED
SCHOOL
SISTER
THIS
TOO
WE
YOU

SIGHT WORDS

- AND
- BAKE
- BEAUTIFUL
- BLUE
- BROTHER
- BROTHERS
- BUT
- CALL
- CAN
- COLOR
- DAD
- DRESS
- EACH
- FAMILY
- FAVORITE
- HANDSOME
- HIM
- HIS

WE LOVE OUR FAMILY
AND EACH OTHER TOO!

WE LOVE GOING TO THE
SAME SCHOOL, AND WE
LOVE TO PLAY FORTNITE!

WE ARE BROTHERS!
WE LOVE BEING BIG BROTHERS!
WE LOVE TO DRESS ALIKE!

SHE IS SMART AND
CAN BE BOSSY TOO!

SHE LOVES US, AND
WE LOVE HER TOO!

OUR SISTER IS PRETTY!

OUR DADDY IS A GREAT DAD,
AND HE CAN DO ANYTHING!

HE LOVES US, AND WE
LOVE HIM TOO!

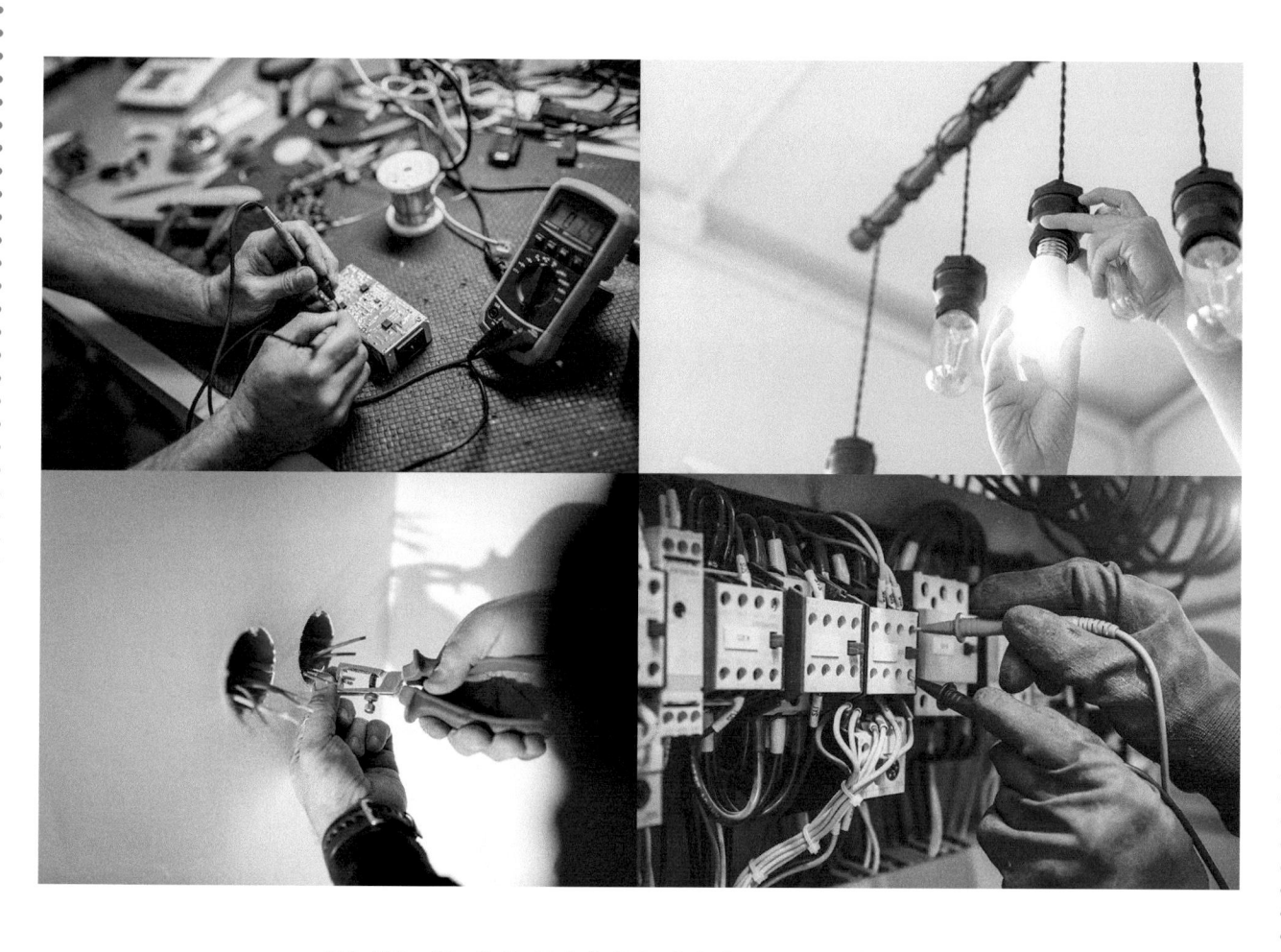

OUR DADDY IS HANDSOME,
AND HE CAN FIX ANY
ELECTRICAL PROBLEM!

OUR MOMMY CAN DO ANYTHING!
SHE COOKS, SHE CLEANS,
AND SHE TAKES CARE OF
US WHEN WE ARE SICK.

SHE LOVES US, AND WE
LOVE HER TOO!

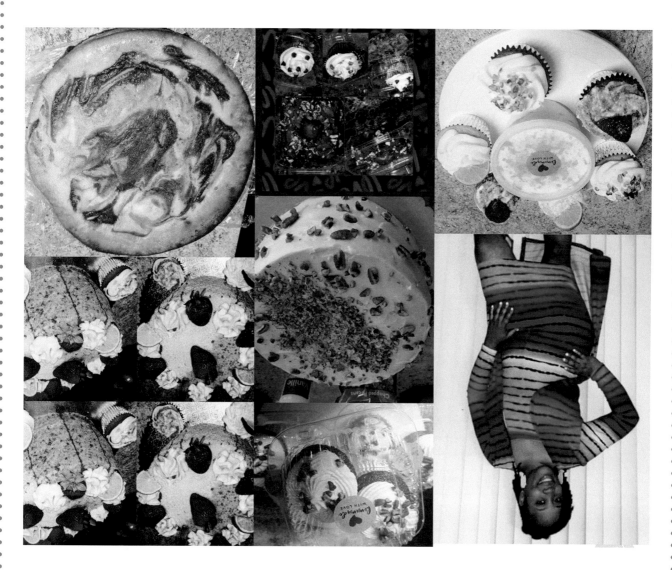

OUR MOMMY IS BEAUTIFUL,
AND SHE LOVES TO BAKE!

WE LOVE OUR FAMILY!

HELLO! WE ARE JARROD & JEREMIAH...